DATE DUE NOV 04

GAYLORD			PRINTED IN U.S.A.

THE
CALIFORNIA PEOPLE

by

LINDA THOMPSON

Rourke

Publishing LLC

Vero Beach, Florida 32964

www.rourkepublishing.com

PHOTO CREDITS:
Library of Congress, Prints & Photographs Division, Edward S. Curtis Collection: cover, title page, pages 6, 9,11-13, 16, 18, 19, 22-28, 31- 33, 35, 37, 38, 43; Andreas Trawny: pages 4, 31; Army Art Collection, U.S. Army Center of Military History: page 7; Courtesy of The Division of Anthropology, American Museum of Natural History (AMNH): pages 9, 16-18, 23-25, 29, 30, 35, 38, 39, 42; Library of Congress, American Folklife Center, WPA Sidney Robertson Cowell Collection: page 11; National Archives and Records Administration: page 14; Fred Marvel: page 15; Courtesy Charles Reasoner: pages 20, 21, 36, 39; Courtesy of the Bancroft Library, University of California, Berkeley: page 30; Courtesy of the National Anthropological Archives, Smithsonian Institution: page 37; Courtesy of the Arizona Department of Tourism: page 40; Courtesy of Ilka Hartmann: page 40.

DESIGN AND LAYOUT by Rohm Padilla, Mi Casa Publications, printing@taosnet.com

Library of Congress Cataloging-In-Publication Data

Thompson, Linda, 1941-
  The California people / by Linda Thompson.
     p. cm. -- (Native peoples, Native lands)
Includes bibliographical references and index.
Contents: The California people today -- Where they came from -- Life in
California -- What they believe.
  ISBN 1-58952-753-4 (hardcover)
  1. Indians of North America--California--History--Juvenile literature.
2. Indians of North America--California--Social life and
customs--Juvenile literature. [1. Indians of North
America--California.] I. Title. II. Series: Thompson, Linda, 1941-
Native peoples, Native lands.
  E78.C15T46 2003
  979.4004'97--dc21
                                  2003011533

Printed in the USA

TITLE PAGE IMAGE:
Smoky day at the Sugar Bowl, Hupa man; photo by Edward S. Curtis.
Each fishing station was the hereditary possession of some family.
Men who owned no station begged the use of one from those who were either
weary of fishing or had enough salmon for their immediate needs.

TABLE OF CONTENTS

Sculpted Rock,
Point Lobos State Preserve,
California

Chapter I:
THE CALIFORNIA PEOPLE

*O*nce, more than 50 **Native American** tribes (sometimes called **American Indians**) lived in the region that is now the state of California. They spoke about 90 languages belonging to six or seven major Native **language "families."** There were probably close to 300,000 people before European explorers, **missionaries**, and settlers arrived. Today, about 45,000 **California People** live in this region, speaking perhaps 20 languages.

The early Californians occupied more than 1,000 miles (1,609 km) of Pacific coast, as well as the wide interior valleys and Sierra Nevada foothills. The climate varies from wet regions in the northwest, where huge redwood trees grow, to very dry deserts in the southeast. Altitudes and temperatures also vary widely. Except for the extreme desert and high mountain areas, many living things flourished. From acorns to seaweed, Natives used more than 500 different kinds of plants and animals for food.

Death Valley, California

Various **tribelets** lived peacefully side by side, with frequent trading and intermarriage. Because they had plenty to eat, people generally were not **nomadic**, like Native Americans elsewhere. High mountain ranges separated them from the Plains and Great Basin Peoples, who had quickly adapted to riding horses brought by Spaniards. Since they did not travel great distances to hunt or raid other tribes, Californian Natives did not have the same need for the horse. They avoided warfare and usually settled quarrels between tribelets or individuals by negotiating.

NORTHWEST & SUBARCTIC

CALIFORNIA

PLATEAU

GREAT BASIN

PLAINS

NORTHEAST WOODLANDS

SOUTHWEST

SOUTHEAST WOODLANDS

ATLANTIC OCEAN

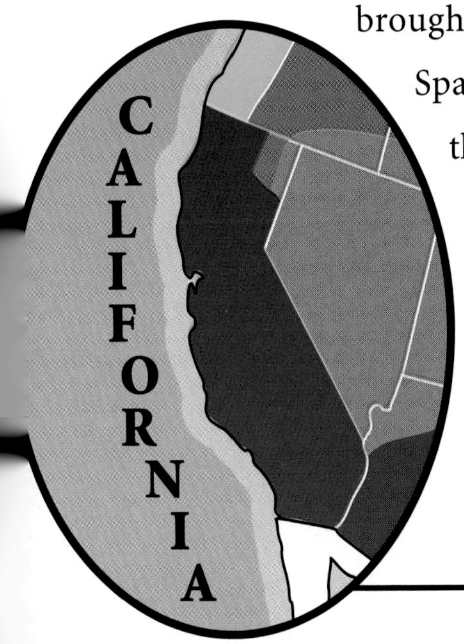

CALIFORNIA

After Christopher Columbus "discovered" America in 1492, European explorers and **immigrants** had an immediate impact on Native tribes in the eastern part of the country. But the lives of California People, far to the west, did not change for nearly three centuries more. Unfortunately, when Europeans did come, the friendly, peaceful nature of California People made it harder for them to resist the invaders. Unlike more warlike tribes, these Natives were not prepared to defend their lands against newcomers who carried guns and rode horses.

(Above) Cahuilla woman with harvest basket and (below) Hupa fisherman

Spain had conquered Mexico very early–in 1519–and Peru soon after that. Led by Juan Rodriguez Cabrillo, the first Spanish explorers sailed up the **Alta California** coast in 1542. Not finding treasure, they did not soon return to colonize the region. But in the 1760s, Russian explorers sailed from the northwest, where they had

The first newcomers came to California for animal furs.

forts. They were interested in the fur trade, especially sea otter pelts. Also, England's Hudson's Bay Company came seeking animal pelts. To protect its claim to the region, Spain decided to establish **missions** along the California coast as it had done in **Baja California**.

Father Junipero Serra led an expedition of Franciscan missionaries and soldiers northward in 1769, founding the first mission at San Diego. By 1823, 21 missions had been built, with about 1,000 Natives living at each. To lure Natives to the missions, the priests offered them gifts. When curious Natives arrived, hoping to trade, the Franciscans insisted that they be baptized into Christianity. Once baptized, they were not allowed to leave.

Spanish frontier soldier

The Franciscans' purpose was to obtain new disciples and also cheap labor. Known as **neophytes**, or "new converts," the Natives were supposed to be at the missions only 10 years. During that time, they would learn European skills, including taking care of cattle and crops, expanding the missions, and making carved altars and artwork. At the end of 10 years, these "**Mission Indians**" were to be given land for farming. Some neophytes would be trained to be priests.

(Above) Spanish priests lured natives to missions with promises of gifts and land and then captured and kept them as slaves. (Below) Spanish style mission

But this promise was never fulfilled. In 1821, Mexico had won its independence from Spain. Suddenly, the regions of New Mexico and California were ruled from Mexico City. Mexican ranchers now wanted the lands that had been promised to Natives. Bowing to their wishes, Mexico closed most of the missions and gave the land to new settlers.

Member of the Pomo at Swamp Lake

During this time, diseases that had arrived with the Europeans, such as **malaria**, smallpox, and measles, were wiping out thousands of Natives. Before 1834, most of the deaths were at the missions. By 1834, nearly two-thirds of the original 300,000 California Natives had died of disease or been killed. Later, as more settlers arrived, these diseases also affected Natives outside of the missions. By 1910, only 16,000 Natives remained in the state.

The Russians had established coastal settlements so they could hunt sea otters. But these sites were where the Pomo fished, gathered clams, and collected bird eggs. Russian soldiers frequently attacked Pomo camps, kidnapping women and children for servants. After the Pomo clashed with settlers in 1850, Army troops slaughtered 188 Pomo men, women, and children. This was the "Bloody Island Massacre."

Salmon spear

Shell necklace

When the missions closed, California People could no longer support themselves in the old ways of hunting and fishing. Their lands had been sold to farmers and ranchers. Herds of cattle increasingly replaced the deer, small game, and native plants that had been so abundant. Natives who tried to remain in their homelands had to steal livestock to eat. If caught, they were severely punished or killed. Most of the mission Natives had no choice but to keep working for the new landowners in exchange for room and board.

In 1846, the United States declared war on Mexico. The result was that the future states of New Mexico, Arizona, and California became part of the United States. But that didn't bring relief to Native people. Within a few years, gold had been discovered in the Sierra Nevada foothills. This change was even harder on many Native tribes than the missions had been.

(Left) herds of cattle replaced the native game that the people had hunted for years and (below) old growth forests gave way to farming pastures and cities.

In 1849, when the gold discovery was announced, miners and prospectors rushed in from all over the world. These **"Forty-niners"** drove Native people from their land or slaughtered them. Some companies hired Natives to mine gold, but paid them very poorly or not at all.

Gold brought "Forty-niners" to California in 1849.

The runoff from mining spoiled game habitats and fishing streams. Dams were built, drying up marshlands. Livestock trampled the **tules**, or marsh grasses, which Native Peoples used in many ways–to make baskets, houses, boats, beds, tools, and clothing. Destruction spread as gold was found in other places. Within a few years, the European population had surpassed the Native population.

"Forty-niner"

Woman gathering tules. Valuable patches of tules were destroyed as the search for gold expanded.

Although slavery was illegal in California, in 1850 the state passed a law that allowed people to enslave Natives and sell them as servants. A few years later, state militias began rounding Natives up and confining them on military **reservations** or small **rancherias** to make way for new settlers. Between 1848 and 1860, at least 5,000 Natives were killed by settlers who wanted them out of the way.

In 1852, 18 **treaties** had been made reserving 8.5 million acres (3.43 million ha) for Natives. Under pressure from California settlers, however, the U.S. Congress never **ratified** them. In 1906, Congress established 54 rancherias for Natives, almost all of them in isolated places that no one else wanted.

White areas indicate some modern reservation locations.

California Shoshone rancheria at Santa Isabel

Today, there are 116 rancherias and reservations in California, ranging from 2 to 25,000 acres (.8 to 10,117 ha) in size. Tribes are still trying to recover from the past two and a half centuries. Many tribes were **terminated** by the U.S. government–that is, recognition was taken away. Tribes such as the Coastal Chumash and the Pinoleville Pomo are still trying to have federal recognition restored. Without it, they cannot benefit from programs, such as healthcare assistance, that were created to help them survive their poverty.

One thing that is very important to Natives on reservations is the concept of **sovereignty.** This means that people living on a reservation have their own laws and tribal organizations, and in many ways are not subject to U.S. or state laws. To Native Americans, sovereignty is not possession of the land but a living relationship between the people and the land that supports them.

California Natives photographed in 1916

In recent times, Natives have found new ways to make this relationship work. For example, reservations have created **casinos** in states where gambling is otherwise illegal. The casinos create jobs and provide money for schools and other programs to raise the standard of living. In some areas, casinos employ non-Natives as well as Native residents.

Today, California has more Native Americans than almost any other state, but many have come from other parts of the country to find work. Most of the 220,657 Native people counted by the 2000 **census** live scattered among the general population. Regardless of where they are, California Natives live in houses, drive cars, watch television, and eat many of the same foods that other Americans eat. Children go to public schools and their parents work at a variety of jobs.

Wherever they live, Natives are actively engaged in preserving their heritage. For example, many craftspeople make baskets using the old methods. Some tribes continue to practice their spiritual customs. And there is new interest among young people in tribal languages, songs, dances, and ceremonies. They understand that by engaging in these things, they can keep their history and values alive. To maintain the closeness they once had, families still come together for **powwows**, rodeos, and story-telling festivals, and they try to take time off from jobs and schools to attend these gatherings.

Powwow dancer

Maidu basket tray

Mabel McKay (1907-1993) was a Pomo basket-weaver. She was also a traditional healer. Although she worked most of her life in a cannery, she was famous for her baskets and taught basket-making to college students. She dreamed her basket designs. Her baskets are in the collections of museums, including the Smithsonian in Washington, D.C.

Through singing, dancing, and basket-making, the California People continue to tell their stories. Although their lives will never be what they once were, together they have managed to keep their traditions alive. These tribes have also produced a number of individuals who have achieved recognition in art, music, film, writing, teaching, and other fields. By listening to their voices, Natives and non-Natives alike can better understand who the California People were—and still are.

Rattlesnake design on Yokut baskets

Chapter II

WHERE THEY CAME FROM

Scientists believe that Native Americans descended from Asian people who walked across land or ice bridges beginning perhaps 30,000 years ago. It is also possible that some came by boat. A land **migration** would have occurred at the Bering Strait, a narrow waterway between Siberia (a part of Russia) and the present state of Alaska. Sea levels might have been lower then, exposing land.

BERING STRAIT

Before settlers arrived, native tools and utensils were made of material that could be found and shaped.

Knife made of chipped stone, wood, cloth, and plant fiber string

Within a few thousand years, descendants of these immigrants had spread across North, Central, and South America. They divided into hundreds of different groups, speaking many languages. There is evidence that in some areas, they hunted huge **mammoths** and other large animals that are now extinct. Some groups lived as nomads, wandering great distances in search of food. If water was plentiful and they could grow food, they settled down. Early California people adapted very well to their environment. They used the natural materials around them to make tools and clothing, to feed themselves, and to build shelters.

Mammoth

Wappo woman gathering grapes
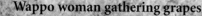

What Do California People Believe About How They Came to America?

The California People have their own stories about how they originated. Most North American tribes believed that the first parents came either from underground or from the sky. In the case of the California tribes, the Creator is seen as residing in the sky or in a faraway corner of the world.

Looking out of painted cave

The Ohlone, or Costanoan, believed that they were created and blessed by **Coyote**. Coyote has a special place in Native lore. Some peoples saw him as a mischievous "trickster." Others gave him god-like powers. When the Ohlone observed Spaniards riding mules, they called them "the children of the Mule." They wondered if an animal-god called "Mule" had created and blessed these strangers just as Coyote had done with them.

Harry Fonseca, born 1946, is part Nisenan Maidu. He has painted the Maidu creation story. Also, he paints Coyote, the "trickster," as a modern character. In 1992, he painted a series called "Discovery of Gold and Souls in California." It represents "the physical, emotional and spiritual genocide of the native people of California" caused by the mission system and later discovery of gold.

**Sea Lion Point,
Point Lobos State Preserve,
California**

One coastal California story tells about two gods, Thunder and Nagaicho, who repaired the old sky by propping it on rocks. They created flowers, clouds, fog, people, the sun and the moon. But floods came and washed it all away. So Nagaicho rode from the north on a great earth dragon. Walking beneath the water, it created land by looking upward. Lying down, the dragon became land itself. Nagaicho created mountains and trees and people with animal names, such as Sea Lion, Grizzly Bear, and Whale. Later, after real people appeared, these early people turned into the animals they were named for. After Nagaicho made food and fresh water to drink, he went back to live in his home in the north.

Yokut woman gathering basket-making supplies

The Luiseño called the creator Chinigchinich [*chin-ig-chin-itch*]. He made the first people out of clay and commanded them to build a temple where they could worship him. If people in trouble ran inside the temple, they would find protection there.

The creation stories told by a tribe or a nation attempt to explain how people and everything else on Earth came into existence. These are just a few among the countless tales that the California People pass from generation to generation to make sure that their history, ancient knowledge, and culture survive.

The Pomo said that Marumba, creator of the world, gave women **kubum**. Kubum is all of the plant materials that go into basket-making. Pomo and other basket-making tribes still see what they create as symbols of their connection with the spiritual world. This story shows how important many California People considered the art of making baskets.

Yokut man at the Tule River Reservation

Chapter III

LIFE IN CALIFORNIA

*O*n the north coast, where redwood trees grew, the Yurok lived in plank houses with small round entrances. They shaped the planks with sharpened elk antlers. In the valleys and foothills, homes might be brush or bark laid over a structure of poles. The Pomo, Miwok, and other tribes of the central coast built

Yurok underground lodge

half-buried houses. A wooden structure over a pit might have a roof covered with earth for insulation. Many tribes built partially buried, mound-shaped assembly lodges or dance houses. Access was through an opening in the roof.

California has many types of native oak trees. **Acorns** from oaks were ground into meal for cooking. In addition, people gathered wild vegetables, **buckeye nuts**, pine nuts, seeds, and grasses. They also dug roots and bulbs, including wild **hyacinths**. Coastal tribes fished with spears, nets, and snares. From beaches and rocks, they collected **abalone, clams,** and **mussels,** as well as **kelp** and seaweed for soup. Tribes that lived near woodlands, lakes, and rivers hunted rabbit, quail, and gophers and caught many types of fish. Desert dwellers ate rabbits, cactus, dates, and insects such as grasshoppers and caterpillars.

(Far left) Abalone shell and (left) acorn nuts

In warmer climates, people wore little clothing. Women wove plant fibers into skirts and stitched deerskin into shirts and dresses. For ceremonies, people wore decorations made of abalone shells and feathers. Northern tribes such as the Yurok made abalone and clam shells into beads, which they used for money. They traded with Plateau Peoples on the Columbia River, as well as with inland tribes, giving beads for **flint**, **obsidian**, and furs.

California People knew how to manage plant life and keep it producing year after year. They were pioneers in conserving resources. For instance, inland Natives who collected wild hyacinth bulbs ate only the large "mother" bulb, carefully replanting the little ones, or "babies." Each spring, the slopes were covered with new flowers, and more bulbs were ready to harvest.

Chipped obsidian shaman talisman

(Left) seed beater and (right) gathering basket

Many

tribes were excellent basket-makers. 5 feet tall (1.5 m) storage baskets held acorns, dried fish, and other food. Women carried **burden baskets** and **"seed-beaters"** into the fields to harvest seeds and acorns. The Pomo made reed canoes at Clear Lake, and other tribes fished from boats made out of tule stalks. Also common were baby cradles and fishing traps made from tule and other fibers. Even hats, belts, and sandals were made from fiber. Both men and women made these items and became skilled at weaving colorful plant fiber and feathers into baskets. The beautiful old creations that are still around sell for very high prices. Also, expert basket-makers continue to teach these traditional skills, often at community colleges.

Burden basket made of woven grass

Gathering seed using handmade basket and seed beater

25

Tribal systems of government were very **democratic**. Each band had a local chief, sometimes called "Big Man" or "captain," who made important decisions and represented his band in tribal council. He could only command others by persuading them that his way was best. Chiefs mainly served as moral examples and spiritual leaders. They also settled arguments and counseled young people. In many tribes, wise **shamans** advised the chief in making decisions.

This Hupa Jumping Dancer's wealth and status are made obvious by his ornate shell necklace.

Although the many bands of California People spoke different languages, they traded with other tribes and sometimes intermarried. If they spoke different languages, the people could still communicate through **sign language**.

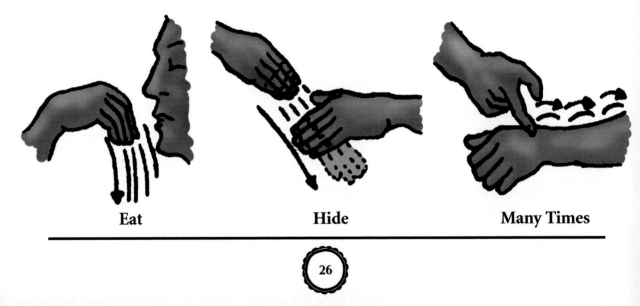

Eat   Hide   Many Times

Joshua trees were one of many sources of wood.

(Above) canoe made out of tules and (below) Yurok man in canoe made from a redwood tree

Some California Tribes

The Yurok and Karok in northern California held "world renewal ceremonies." These featured special dances aimed at renewing the harvest of salmon and game. They wore shells in many different ways and used shells for money. The Karok wore buckskin aprons and moccasins. They hunted with strong bows made from the **yew** tree and wooden arrows tipped with flint or obsidian, carried in a fur quiver. The Yurok made canoes from hollowed-out redwood trees.

The Pomo lived around Clear Lake, a large natural lake north of San Francisco, and along the coast north of Sonoma County. They hunted sea lions, otters, and bears using bows and arrows. Because of Europeans' aggression and diseases, the Pomo were homeless by 1900. They had to work on settlers' ranches just for food and shelter. They number about 5,000 today, mostly on small rancherias in Sonoma, Lake, and Mendocino counties.

Winter house of the Lake Pomo with its tule-covered framework of willow poles

The Yokut, who live around the present city of Fresno, had up to 50 different tribes and dialects. They made rafts and barges from tule stalks. They numbered more than 18,000 in 1770, but now have only about 2,000 members.

Bones were used for gambling long before casinos.

The Serrano, or San Manuel band of Mission Indians, lived near the San Bernardino Mountains and adjacent deserts. They call themselves "Yuhaviatam," [*you-ha-via-tam*] which means "people of the pines." In 1891, when the San Manuel Reservation was set aside for them, only a few hundred were left. They struggled to make a living in their mountainous, infertile land. The future became brighter in the mid-1980s with the creation of a casino. Now, the San Manuel Indian Bingo and Casino is one of the largest employers in the region, with 1,500 employees.

Beads were used as a monetary and trade source before settlers arrived.

(Left) Ishi, the last survivor of the Yana people.
(Below) bow made of wood and sinew

On August 29, 1911, when Oroville residents thought Native Americans had vanished from the Sierra Nevada wilderness, a Yahi man of the Yana People walked into town. Scientists called him Ishi, which in Yahi means "person." He was the last member of his tribe. He became caretaker of the University of California Museum of Anthropology in San Francisco. He taught visitors and scientists his language and traditional crafts. Thanks to Ishi, people learned about the Yahi and the Yana.

The Maidu lived in the central valley between Susanville and Auburn. They held **Kuksu** ceremonies, in which they impersonated their ancestors by wearing colorful costumes. Their houses were bark- or brush-covered lean-to structures. From 9,000 in 1846, their population had declined to 2,500 by 1990. Now they live on small rancherias. They still perform the Maidu Bear Dance every spring at Jamesville.

Maidu headdress made of hawk feathers

Maidu rattle made of cocoons, wood, and sinew

The Miwok lived in 100 villages from the coast north of San Francisco to the Sierra Nevada foothills. There were about 22,000 in three branches during the late 1700s. Now, about 3,400 descendants are scattered throughout their former lands.

Miwok man

Miwok basket-maker

Sierra Nevada Mountains in northern California

Man fishing from carved canoe

The Ohlone are also known as Costanoan (an English version of the Spanish *costeño*, or "coast people"). They inhabited the central coast around Monterey and Carmel. Their descendants have combined with others to form the Costanoan-Rumsen-Carmel People.

The Chumash, also on the central coast, were a large and powerful group. Once 15,000, there are now only several hundred. They snared seals and otters, built canoes, and made shell bead jewelry. The federal government recognizes only one division of the Chumash, the Santa Ynez Band. Its 213 members own and operate a prosperous casino.

This home at Palm Springs shows how Native building styles were influenced by newcomers.

Rattlesnake

The Cahuilla, who lived near what is now Palm Springs, have a rich ceremonial life in which they celebrate their relationship to all things, not only nature but the "sacred past and present." Early members ate palm dates, rabbits, insects, and cactus, which they boiled in stews. From 6,000 or so, their population fell to 1,000 in the 1880s. In 1990, there were about 2,300, including those of mixed ancestry.

Cahuilla basket-maker

Saguaro cactus

Cricket

Chapter IV:
WHAT THEY BELIEVE

All Native peoples' calendars, religion, and legends are based on nature. Their lives once depended entirely upon the earth. To them, everything on earth has a spiritual purpose and everything is interconnected. Although they may have adapted to new ways and new religions, the old faith remains alive. Their belief that nature is sacred is evident in their teachings, writings, art, and culture. It is passed from generation to generation through stories and ceremonies.

White Deerskin dancer

Northern California Peoples such as the Hupa, Yurok, and Karok celebrated autumn with a ceremony for "world renewal." These dances assured a successful hunting and fishing season, and some are still danced today. In the White Deerskin Dance, dancers carried the dried remains of rare albino deer. In the Boat Dance, they danced–while standing in dugout canoes–to restore harmony on earth. The canoe moved to and from shore, suggesting a movement between the land of the living and the land of the dead. In the Jump Dance, people wore headdresses made of red woodpecker scalps and white deerskin. Today, the Yurok dance the *May-loh* (Brush Dance) to help the Medicine Woman cure a sick child.

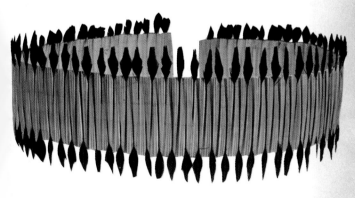

Traditional dancer with feather hat

Wild blueberries

Like other Natives, California Peoples believe in the "sacred hoop" or circle. This refers not only to physical circles but also to the cycles of life. When seasons change and the stars, planets, sun, and moon seem to move across the sky, it is part of the never-ending circle. The familiar seasonal changes from fishing and hunting to gathering tule stalks and berries is also a circle. And each generation growing from infancy to adulthood to old age is another.

This circle is also called the **Medicine Wheel**. Some tribes such as the Achumawi [*achoo-ma-wee*] built piles of stones in a circle, making a prayer circle. To go there and pray, a person had to first be purified by a shaman to ward off evil spirits.

A medicine wheel represents the circle of life and many other natural events, such as compass directions, seasons, and elements.

Some California People honored their ancestors through Kuksu ceremonies. Young people were initiated through **ghost rituals**. Later, some features from other parts of the country were added, including the **Ghost Dance of 1870**, the **Earth Lodge Cult**, and the **Bole-Maru Dream Dance**.

White Deerskin dancer

Diegueño dancers

Native people felt their deceased ancestors were still among them. This is one reason it was so hard for tribes to leave their homelands. When a rancher forced the Cupeño from their ancestral lands in San Diego County, their chief said, "We would rather die here. Our fathers did. We cannot leave them. Our children were born here. How can we go away?" But their land had been sold, and they were forced to leave.

The California People believe that personal spirits guide them through life. **Visions** are important to both men and women. In the past, men helped boys have visions by giving them a strong drink made from the **jimson** weed. A person with a lot of spiritual power might become a shaman, or healer.

Female shaman

Shamans led hunting rituals and ceremonies and presided over burials, among other duties. Often, the idea of being a shaman came to people in their dreams. In California, many shamans were women. For Mission Indians, forced to convert to Christianity, the tribal shaman helped them stay connected to their traditional beliefs. They often combined Christian ceremonies with their ancient ones.

Herbs like this wild nutmeg, and plants of all types, were used for religious ceremonies, healing, and medicinal purposes.

(Above) illustration of a ceremonial tobacco pipe. (Right) small tobacco pipe with leather pouch

Native peoples once used **tobacco** as a sacred ceremonial plant. In tobacco ceremonies, smoke is considered a type of prayer. A pipe ceremony might be held to heal someone, whether present, far away, or deceased. Hunters may smoke a pipe together to show respect for the animals that have died to feed them. The sacred uses of tobacco differ, but California Peoples agree that tobacco should be used for prayer, protection, respect, and healing.

Holding powwows is an ancient tradition among Native peoples. Though in some cultures the powwow was a religious event, today it is more of a social occasion. However, ceremonies and other religious observances may also be part of the powwow, which includes dancing, singing, feasting, and honoring old friendships.

Last occupier to leave Alcatraz. Photo by Ilka Hartmann © 2003

The island of Alcatraz in San Francisco Bay was once a hiding place for Native Americans who escaped the missions. Later, it was a federal prison, and today it is a tourist attraction. But in 1969, Alcatraz became a symbol of Native American independence. A group calling themselves "Indians of All Tribes" arrived to symbolically claim the island for their people. On June 10, 1971, the occupation ended. But as a result, the government began letting Natives have a voice in their future.

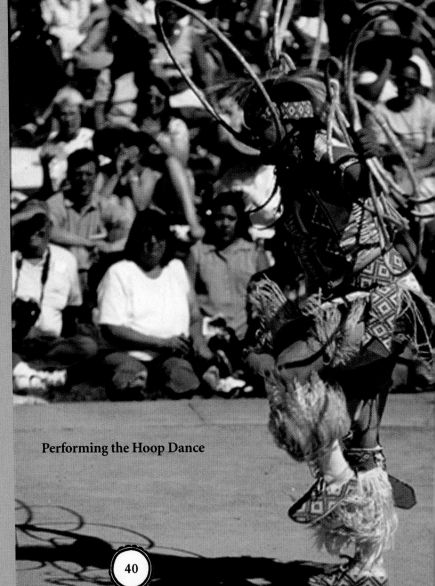

Performing the Hoop Dance

Early Native peoples could not understand the European view that the earth is something that could be bought and sold. When settlers cut down forests for houses, dammed rivers, plowed up the earth to plant crops, and fenced off the land to keep others out, Natives were shocked. Today, many Native people are committed to healing the damage to the natural environment caused by "civilization."

For instance, in 1979, when the Army Corps of Engineers planned a major dam in a place where valuable grasses grew, Pomo basket-weavers got involved. They wanted to transplant the grasses and **sedge** where they would flourish. The result was a new Native plant nursery. It is a place for environmental learning and the preservation of sacred plants. This was an example of Native people teaching environmental protection that is in tune with their ancient values.

Examples of trees found in California

King salmon

Salmon catching basket

In the Native worldview, everything is interrelated. Thus, Native Americans were early **ecologists**–people who study relationships between **organisms** and their environment. Natives have always been dedicated to the conservation of nature, to recycling natural resources, and to ensuring a healthy world for future generations. In their view, humans are a part of nature, not a superior creature meant to dominate it.

Once, the survival of Native tribes depended on having strong, brave warriors, so ceremonies were held to honor warriors' deeds. Today, that feeling is kept alive in the respect shown to veterans of U.S. wars. Large numbers of Native men and women have served in the Armed Forces. Native Americans have fought for the United States in every war. Today, powwows and tribal ceremonies often include flag songs and similar observances for Native veterans.

Each summer a fishing weir was built across the river.
From a platform, fish were caught using a dipnet or
spear. Rising spring waters washed the
structure away. Since building a
weir was a community project,
the catch was divided
according to need.

A TIMELINE OF THE HISTORY OF
THE CALIFORNIA PEOPLE

30,000 to 13,000 BC - Ice ages lower sea levels, making it possible for people to walk across a land bridge from Asia to North America.

12,000 to 9,000 BC - Earth warms up and the ice caps melt, allowing people to move throughout North, Central, and South America.

8000 BC to AD 1400 - People who speak languages belonging to the Hokan and Yukian families arrive in the south and along the coast. Eventually, bands speaking four other main language families join them in the region. These peoples evolve into a "crazy quilt" of cultures speaking more than 90 languages and 300 dialects.

AD 1492 - Christopher Columbus arrives in America near present-day Florida. Thinking he is in India, he names the inhabitants "Indians."

AD 1519 to 1531 - Spain conquers the Aztec Empire of Mexico and the Inca Empire of Peru.

AD 1542 - Juan Rodriguez Cabrillo sails into San Diego harbor, becoming the first European to enter California.

AD 1769 - Father Junipero Serra, Franciscan friar with the Gaspar de Portola expedition, establishes the first California mission near present-day San Diego.

AD 1776 - The American Revolution creates a new country, the U.S.A.

AD 1804 - Spain divides California into Alta ("high") and Baja ("low") California. Monterey becomes the capital of Alta California.

AD 1804 to 1806 - The Lewis and Clark Expedition explores western lands from St. Louis to the mouth of the Columbia River.

AD 1821 - Mexico wins independence from Spain and Alta and Baja California become parts of Mexico.

AD 1846 - The United States declares war on Mexico.

AD 1848 to 1850 - The Treaty of Guadalupe Hidalgo ends the Mexican War, making Alta California part of the United States. On September 9, 1850, that region becomes the state of California. Baja California remains a Mexican province.

AD 1849 - Gold is discovered in the Sierra Nevada foothills.

AD 1861 to 1865 - The American Civil War is fought, with California a "Union" State (on the side of the North). The war ends with the abolition of slavery.

AD 1870 - Of the 200,000 or 300,000 Natives who once lived in California, fewer than 30,000 remain.

AD 1969 to 1971 - Indians of All Tribes take over Alcatraz, an abandoned federal prison in San Francisco Bay, calling public attention to the plight of Native Americans.

GLOSSARY

abalone - An edible single-shelled mollusk (clam-like animal) that clings to rocks.

acorn - The nut of the oak tree.

Alta California - Spanish for "upper California."

American Indian - A member of the first peoples of North America.

Baja California - Spanish for "lower California."

Bole-Maru Dream Dance - A dance in which spirits of the dead were asked to heal the cultural and spiritual damage of Natives.

buckeye nut - The nut-like seed of a tree of the horse chestnut family.

burden basket - A basket made to sling over the back or shoulders for carrying goods.

California People - Natives of what is now most of the state of California.

casino - A building used for gambling.

census - A count of the population of an area.

clam - An edible mollusk, or sea animal, with two shells, which lives in sand or mud.

Coyote - A North American member of the canine family, smaller than a wolf.

democratic - Relating to government by the people, especially the rule of the majority.

Earth Lodge Cult - A religious practice in which the end of the world was predicted.

ecologist - A scientist who studies the relationships between organisms and their environment.

flint - A type of hard rock.

Forty-niner - A person taking part in the California Gold Rush of 1849.

Ghost Dance of 1870 - A dance in which a train would bring the spirits of deceased Natives back to reclaim their land.

ghost ritual - A type of dance or initiation ceremony that called upon the spirits of the dead for blessings.

hyacinth - A plant of the lily family with a bulb-like root and fragrant flowers.

immigrant - A person who comes to a country to live in it.

jimson - A poisonous tall weed of the nightshade family.

kelp - A type of large, brown seaweed.

kubum - Pomo word for the sacred plant materials used to make baskets.

Kuksu - One name for the Creator in the Pomo dialect.

language family - A group of languages related to each other by similarities in vocabulary, grammar, and pronunciation.

malaria - Disease caused by parasites in the red blood cells and carried by mosquitoes.

mammoth - Extinct hairy elephants living about 1,600,000 years ago.

Medicine Wheel - The concept that the "power of the world" moves in a circle.

migration - The movement of a person or group from one country or place to another.

mission - A church surrounded by a settlement, built for the purpose of converting the residents to a given faith.

Mission Indian - The Native converts who helped build and maintain the Spanish missions and lived nearby.

missionary - One who goes on assignment to convert people to one's beliefs or religion.

mussel - An edible mollusk (clam-like animal) with a dark, oval shell.

Native American - A synonym for American Indian.

neophyte - A new convert.

nomadic - People who move from place to place and have no fixed residence.

obsidian - A dark natural glass formed when lava cools.

organism - A living being.

powwow - Originally referred to a shaman, a vision, or a gathering. Now, it means a cultural, social, and spiritual gathering to celebrate Native culture and pride.

rancheria - Spanish for "small ranch."

ratify - To formally approve.

reservation - A tract of public land set aside for a specific use. Tracts set aside for Natives. In Canada, they are called "reserves."

sedge - A tufted marsh plant.

seed-beater - Slightly scooped basket-like tool used to knock seeds from grasses.

shaman Medicine man or woman.

sign language A formal language that uses hand gestures instead of words.

sovereignty Independent power and freedom from outside control.

terminate To end something.

tobacco - Native American plant that belongs to the nightshade family.

treaty - An agreement or arrangement, usually written, made by negotiating.

tribelet - A subdivision of a tribe, sometimes called "band."

tule - A type of large, tufted marsh plant.

vision A perception that a young Native seeks when going on a "vision quest," which will guide him or her through life.

yew - A type of evergreen tree or shrub.

Books of Interest

Bean, Lowell Jordan and Lisa J. Bourgealt. *The Cahuilla.* New York: Chelsea House, 1989.

Bee, Robert L. *The Yuma.* New York: Chelsea House, 1989.

Erdoes, Richard and Alfonso Ortiz, eds. *American Indian Myths and Legends.* New York: Pantheon, 1984

Gibson, Robert O. *The Chumash.* New York: Chelsea House, 1991.

Johnson, Michael. *Encyclopedia of Native Tribes of North America.* New York: Gramercy Books, 2001.

La Farge, Oliver. *The American Indian.* New York: Golden Press, 1956.

Nerburn, Kent, ed. *The Wisdom of the Native Americans.* Novato, Calif.: New World Library, 1999.

Patterson, Victoria, DeAnna Barney, Les Lincoln, and Skip Willits, eds. *The Singing Feather: Tribal Remembrances from Round Valley.* Ukiah: Mendocino County Library, 1990.

Trafzer, Clifford E. *California's Indians and the Gold Rush.* Sacramento: Sierra Oaks Publishing Company, 1989.

Woodhead, Henry, series ed. *The American Indians.* Alexandria: Time Life Inc., 1992-94.

Children's Atlas of Native Americans. Chicago: Rand McNally & Co., 1996.

Good Web Sites to Begin Researching Native Americans

General Information Site with Links
http://www.nativeculture.com

Resources for Indigenous Cultures around the World
http://www.nativeweb.org/

Index of Native American Resources on the Internet
http://www.hanksville.org/NAresources/

News and Information from a Native American Perspective
http://www.indianz.com

An Online Newsletter Celebrating Native America
http://www.turtletrack.org

Native American History in the United States
http://web.uccs.edu/~history/index/nativeam.html

Internet School Library Media Center
http://falcon.jmu.edu/~ramseyil/native.htm

University Web Sites with California Native Resources
California State University at Long Beach
http://www.csulb.edu/projects/ais/

University of California at Berkeley
http://www.mip.berkeley.edu/cilc/bibs/toc.html

INDEX

Linda Thompson is a Montana native and a graduate of the University of Washington. She has been a teacher, writer, and editor in the San Francisco Bay Area for 30 years and now lives in Taos, New Mexico. She can be contacted through her web site, http://www.highmesaproductions.com